* WE ARE AMERICA *

Thai Americans

KAREN PRICE HOSSELL

Heinemann Library
Chicago, Illinois

Designed by Roslyn Broder
Photo research by Scott Braut
Printed in China by WKT Company Limited

08 07 06 05 04
10 9 8 7 6 5 4 3 2 1

Library of Congress Cataloging-in-Publication Data
Price Hossell, Karen, 1957-
   Thai Americans / Karen Price Hossell.
      p. cm. -- (We are America)
   Summary: An overview of the history and daily lives of Thai people who immigrated to the
   United States.
   Includes bibliographical references (p.   ) and index.
   ISBN 1-4034-5025-0
   1. Thai Americans--History--Juvenile literature. 2. Thai Americans--Social life and customs--
Juvenile literature. [1. Thai Americans.] I. Title. II. Series.
   E184.T4P75 2004
   973'.0495911--dc22
                                    2003021705

Acknowledgments
The author and publisher are grateful to the following for permission to reproduce copyright
material: pp. 4, 5, 28, 29 Courtesy of Dee Debhavalya; pp. 7, 8 Horace Bristol/Corbis; p. 9 Hulton
Archive/Getty Images; p. 10 Katrina Thomas/City Lore; pp. 12, 13 Michael Newman/Photo Edit;
p. 14 Jennifer Szymaszek/AP Wide World Photos; p. 15 Paula Bronstein/Liaison; pp. 16, 17, 21 Nick
Ut/AP Wide World Photos; p. 18 John Ewing/Portland Press Herald/AP Wide World Photo; pp. 19, 25,
27 David Young-Wolff/Photo Edit; p. 20 Mike Fiala/NewsCom; p. 22 Kelly-Mooney Photography/
Corbis; p. 23 Brian Leatart/FoodPix; p. 24 Charles Dharapak/AP Wide World Photo; p. 26 Rommell
Pecson/The Image Works

Cover photographs by Michael Newman/Photo Edit

Special thanks to Dee Debhavalya for her comments made in preparation of this book. Karen Price
Hossell would like to thank Brian Krumm and Dee Debhavalya for sharing her story.

Some quotations and material used in this book come from the following source. In some cases,
quotes have been abridged for clarity: p. 16 Smithsonian Institute.

Every effort has been made to contact copyright holders of any material reproduced in this book.
Any omissions will be rectified in subsequent printings if notice is given to the publisher.

A Thai-American family who lives in Los Angeles, California, is shown on the cover of this
book. A photo of the Thai Town area in Los Angeles is shown in the background.

Contents

Some words are shown in bold, **like this.** You can
find out what they mean by looking in the glossary.

From Bangkok to Chicago

Dee Debhavalya moved to the United States from Thailand in 1970 to go to college. She planned to study computers, get her **degree,** and return to Thailand to work. Dee's cousin lived in Chicago, Illinois, so at first Dee stayed with her. Dee thought she would like the U.S. because she had seen many American movies. She thought it looked like a fun place to live.

This photo of Dee was taken in South Carolina in 1977.

However, even though she was from Bangkok, the biggest city in Thailand, it was hard for Dee to get used to living in Chicago. It helped that some people in Chicago were kind to her. One day, she fell on an icy sidewalk, and two people helped her get up. Soon, Dee started to feel more comfortable in the U.S. After attending college in South Carolina, Dee was offered a job in Chicago. When her mother decided to move to the U.S. from Thailand, Dee decided to stay in the U.S.

Dee graduated from Francis Marion University in Florence, South Carolina.

When I came to Chicago in July, I was surprised that it stayed light so late into the evening. I did not know about **daylight saving time**. Boy, was I surprised when the winter came. Not only did it get dark early, but the weather was so cold. It never gets that cold in Thailand!

—Dee Debhavalya

Thailand

Thailand is a country in Southeast Asia. It is about the same size as the state of Alaska. Thailand is a very warm country and is sometimes very rainy. The word *Thailand* means "land of the free" in the Thai language. Many people in Thailand know how to speak English because they study English in school.

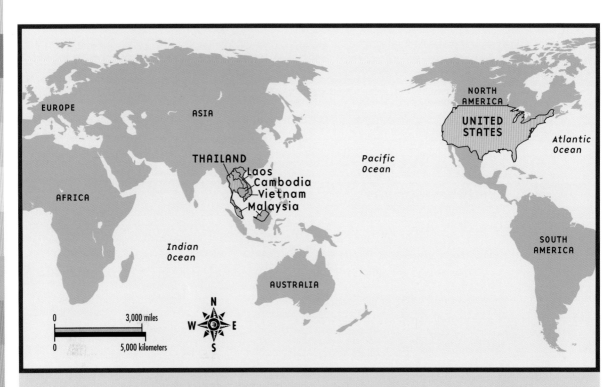

This map shows where the U.S. and Thailand are located. Thailand is located near the countries of Malaysia, Cambodia, Vietnam, and Laos.

This photo from about 1950 shows boats at a market in Bangkok, Thailand's capital city.

Thai people began to move to the United States in large numbers in the 1960s. Many Thai people **immigrated** to attend U.S. schools. Getting **degrees** in the U.S. would help them get good jobs back in Thailand. Many Thai professionals, or workers such as doctors and lawyers, also immigrated during this time. They found they could make much more money in the U.S. Others left Thailand because they felt that the way of life in the U.S. was more relaxed than in Thailand.

Deciding to Leave Thailand

Until the 1960s, not many people left Thailand to go to the United States. One reason was that government leaders in the U.S. passed a law in 1917. The law kept all Asians except Japanese people from **immigrating** to the U.S. That law was changed in 1952, but still not many Thai people immigrated. Most were happy living in Thailand. There was enough food for everyone, and there were no disasters, such as **earthquakes.**

One reason not many Thai people left Thailand was because there was enough food for everyone. These Thai workers are shown collecting rice in about 1950.

What Was the Vietnam War?

The **Vietnam War** lasted from 1955 to 1975. The country of Vietnam used to be divided into two parts, north and south. North Vietnam's government leaders wanted to take over South Vietnam. The U.S. sent soldiers to help South Vietnam fight against forces from the north. However, North Vietnam ended up taking over the south.

In the 1960s and 1970s, soldiers were fighting a war in Vietnam, a country near Thailand. The U.S. government set up military bases in Thailand. Some Thai people met and married American soldiers during the war and later moved to the U.S. with them. Like earlier immigrants, Thai people also went to the U.S. during this time to earn college **degrees** and to work. Some planned to go back to Thailand. But many found that they liked living in the U.S. Students were often offered good jobs when they graduated from college.

These people went to the U.S. by boat in 1975 to get away from the Vietnam War. Many others escaped the war by traveling to Thailand. Some of them later moved to the U.S. from Thailand.

9

Settling in the United States

Many Thai **immigrants** chose to live in cities in the United States where the weather was warm like it is in Thailand. Los Angeles, San Francisco, Miami, and Tampa are some of the cities in which they **settled.** So many Thai people settled in an area in Los Angeles that it became known as Thai Town. There are many Thai restaurants, shops, and art galleries there. About 75,000 Thai Americans live in California, and thousands more live in Florida, Texas, and other states across the U.S.

This photo shows a group of Thai Americans who live in New York. The two persons wearing orange robes are **Buddhist monks.**

Thai Immigration to the United States

This map shows some of the cities and states that Thai people first moved to and where many of them still live today.

Time Line

1917 — The U.S. government passes a law that keeps Thai people and other Asians from immigrating to the United States.

1955–1975 — The **Vietnam War** is fought. The U.S. uses military bases in Thailand during the war. Some American soldiers meet and marry Thai people and bring them to the U.S.

1965 — Immigration laws are changed to allow almost anyone to immigrate to the U.S.

1960s–1970s — Thais begin immigrating to the U.S. to look for school and job opportunities.

2000 — About 150,000 people from Thailand make their homes in the U.S.

Living in the United States

Thai **immigrants** have to face many challenges when they begin living in the United States. For example, Thai students might have to get used to what is considered to be normal conduct in classrooms. Thai students might be shy about asking questions. In Thailand, asking questions is thought of as being impolite. Some Thai students might prefer to ask questions in private, away from other people.

Americans often ask, "How are you?" In Thailand, we would give a long answer to this question. We think that someone who asks this wants to know exactly how we are doing. But in the United States, no one expects you to give a long answer to this. They might act bored, amused, or even frightened by our answer.

—Dr. Poranee Natadech-Sponsel, a Thai-American professor at Chaminade University of Honolulu, Hawaii

This Thai-American girl gave a report to her class in Los Angeles. Many Thai Americans her age were born in the U.S.

Thai immigrants and Thai Americans born in the U.S. celebrate American holidays that they might not celebrate in Thailand. This Thai-American family is shown enjoying a Thanksgiving meal.

Thai immigrants also have to get used to other differences in the U.S. For example, Thai Americans must learn to drive on the right side of the road. In Thailand, people drive on the left side. Immigrants must also get used to new types of food and clothing.

Many Thai immigrants learn English after they move to the U.S. Others already know how to speak English. Here are some English words along with how to say the words in the Thai language.

English	Thai	English	Thai
hello	*sawatdee khrab* (if you are a boy) *sawatdee kaa* (if you are a girl)		
beach	*haat*	egg	*khay*
car	*rot-yon*	bird	*nok*
house	*baan*	water	*nam*

Thoughts of Thailand

The lives of most Thai Americans are not very different from those of other Americans. Thai Americans go to school or work, watch movies, and have hobbies. Many Thai Americans also like to do things that remind them of life back in Thailand. For example, some Thai Americans like to cook Thai food. In their own gardens, they grow the same kinds of fruits and vegetables that they could find at markets in Thailand.

In Thailand, beautiful designs are often carved into fruit before it is served. These women carved watermelons as part of a Thai Day festival in New York.

Kickboxing is a popular sport in Thailand. Some Thai-American boys and girls kickbox in the U.S. These Thai female kickboxers competed in a match in 2000.

Some Thai Americans also play sports that remind them of home. The most popular sport in Thailand is probably soccer. At Stanford University in California, Thai-American students have formed a club that plays soccer often. Thai boxing, or kickboxing, and **martial arts** are also popular.

> Thai people like to grow vegetables because they come from an **agricultural** country. They like to use the land.
> —Dee Debhavalya

15

Illegal Immigrants

In the 1980s and 1990s, some people from Thailand were brought into the United States as **illegal immigrants.** They were promised good jobs and nice places to live. The workers sometimes had to pay their **employers** up to $5,000 for helping them get jobs. Many of these Thai workers ended up working in factories in California.

> I really miss Thailand. If I knew it would be like this, I wouldn't have decided to come here. . . . Samli, please tell me what to do. Sometimes I really think about running away from here.
>
> —Kijja Pimolsing, a Thai sweatshop worker, from a letter to a friend in Thailand

Some Thai immigrants were forced to work in shops like this one in Los Angeles.

These Thai women were among 72 workers who were forced to sew clothing in a sweatshop in California. This photo shows them after they were freed from the shop in August 1995.

Many of these factories were called sweatshops because they were hot and had few or no windows and no air conditioning. Workers were forced to work long, hard hours for very low pay. Guards watched them so they did not try to escape.

In 1995, government agents closed down a sweatshop in California. Thai immigrants had been forced to work there for about seven years. The workers had to work up to eighteen hours per day for only $1.60 per hour. Their case led to the creation of a new law to protect immigrant workers.

Jobs

Today, Thai Americans work at many kinds of jobs. There are Thai-American doctors, lawyers, nurses, teachers, and writers. Most Thai Americans think that education is important. Young people do not usually take jobs until they finish school. Some Thai Americans own or work in Thai-food restaurants. Most major cities have several Thai restaurants. Even some smaller towns have one or two.

Thai American Suwanna Truong is the owner of a Thai-food restaurant in Portland, Maine. She opened the restaurant in 2003.

This Thai-American woman works at a medical library in a hospital. Medical libraries have books that are most often used by doctors and nurses.

Thai Americans have formed **associations** to help one another. Some of these associations, such as the Thai American Young Professionals Association (TAYPA), have offices all over the United States. Members share information about working in the U.S. and organize dinners and dances.

Ruangsung "Joe" Wana of San Francisco started TAYPA. He started it "to fill the needs of people like myself—Thais born in the U.S.—so that we would not lose the Thai community that existed here. And we could continue the Thai **heritage** for the next generations to come."

Family Life

Family life is very important to most Thai Americans. Thai-American children are expected to treat other family members, especially older people, with respect. They are often taught to be polite and quiet around all adults. Thai-American children also usually have duties and tasks to do around the house.

Kultida Punsawad Woods, a Thai American, is the mother of one of the most famous Americans in the world, golfer Tiger Woods. Kultida met Tiger's father, Earl Woods, in Thailand's capital city of Bangkok. They were married in 1969.

*Many Thai-American parents follow **Buddhism** and teach their children about the religion. These Thai Americans in Los Angeles support **monks** who live in the area by giving them food.*

In Thai-American homes, older children are expected to help take care of their younger brothers and sisters. As soon as they are old enough, children are also expected to help out with chores around the house. If the family owns a business, older children usually help out with that as well.

Many Thai Americans are Buddhists. The Buddhist religion teaches that peace and happiness can be found by getting rid of your desire to own things in the world. Today, there are more than 100 Thai **temples** in the United States.

Thai Food

Thai food is very popular in the United States. Many kinds of Thai food are available. People who came from different parts of Thailand brought local flavors with them to the U.S. Someone who came from the south of Thailand would be used to eating more fish and other seafood than someone from the north. That is because southern Thailand borders the sea.

This Thai-American woman works in a Thai-food restaurant in New York City. She is holding several Thai dishes.

These are some of the dishes that might be available at a Thai restaurant.

People from the northeastern part of Thailand, near the country of Laos, are used to very spicy food. Many Thai Americans like food that is hot and spicy. They cook with hot peppers, which make the food spicy. Thai meals also include servings of fruits, vegetables, and salad.

Thai Words for Food

khaaw	rice
man farang	potato
chaa	tea
plaa	fish
kluay	banana

Celebrations and Traditions

Thai Americans celebrate many different holidays and events. Because some of their **ancestors** came from China, many Thai Americans celebrate Chinese New Year. This occurs around the end of January or beginning of February and lasts for two weeks. Americans of many different backgrounds attend parades and festivals to observe Chinese New Year.

These Thai-American girls from Maryland and Washington, D.C., performed traditional Thai dances at a Thai festival in 2003.

These Thai-American girls performed in costumes as part of a Thai New Year's festival. It was held in Los Angeles.

On April 13, Thai Americans celebrate *Songkran,* which is the Thai New Year. Because April is a hot time of year in Thailand, it is a **tradition** on Thai New Year to throw water on people for fun. It is also a time for young people to show respect for older people by giving them gifts, such as flowers or clothing.

There are generations of Thai Americans who were born in the United States. As a result, Thai Americans are likely to celebrate traditional American holidays, such as Independence Day, as well as Thai holidays.

25

Thai Dancing and Music

Traditional Thai dancing uses fancy costumes and masks. The masks are covered with jewels. One kind of dance is called the *khon*. Usually, men wearing different masks do this dance. Many areas of Thailand also have their own **folk** dances. One of these dances is called the *ramwong*.

*This Thai-American girl danced as part of a festival in New York City in 2001. The festival was held to showcase the **cultures** and traditions that immigrants brought to the United States.*

These Thai-American women played Thai musical instruments in a parade during a Thai New Year's celebration.

Traditional Thai music uses several different instruments. One is a type of wooden xylophone called the *ranart*. Thai musicians also use gongs and **cymbals.** To keep time, they often use two *ching*. These are small metal instruments that musicians bang together. They might also play another type of cymbal called a *mong*. A *mong* gets its name from the sound it makes when played.

A New Home

Dee Debhavalya knew she wanted to remain in the United States when she got a good job and her mother came to live with her. In 1983, she married her husband, John. Today, Dee, John, and Dee's mother live near Chicago, Illinois. Dee has become used to the cold Illinois weather in the winter and now thinks Thailand is too hot. She has gone back to Thailand to visit a few times and see family members. She plans to stay in the U.S.

*Dee met her husband John in Chicago. She is seen here with John at a party organized by her **employers** in about 1990.*

The thing Dee likes most about living in the U.S. is the freedom to be herself. She believes that people are more accepting in the U.S. than in Thailand and that there are not so many rules about how people should act. Like many other Thai Americans, Dee likes living in the U.S. because it has become her home.

Dee is seen here with her mother and half brother during a trip to Thailand. At the time the photo was taken, she had not been to Thailand in about 15 years.

One thing I like about being an American is that you have the right to vote for who will lead your country. And if you don't agree with that leader, you can criticize him in public.
—Dee Debhavalya

Thai Immigration Chart

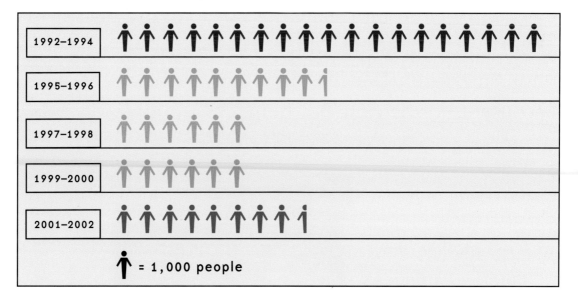

1992–1994	🚹🚹🚹🚹🚹🚹🚹🚹🚹🚹🚹🚹🚹🚹🚹🚹🚹🚹🚹🚹🚹🚹
1995–1996	🚹🚹🚹🚹🚹🚹🚹🚹🚹
1997–1998	🚹🚹🚹🚹🚹🚹
1999–2000	🚹🚹🚹🚹🚹
2001–2002	🚹🚹🚹🚹🚹🚹🚹🚹

🚹 = 1,000 people

*It is not known for sure how many Thai **immigrants** came to the United States before the 1990s. This chart shows how many Thai immigrants came to the U.S. from 1992–2002.*

Source: U.S. Immigration and Naturalization Service

More Books to Read

Boraas, Tracey. *Thailand.* Mankato, Minn.: Capstone Press, 2002.

Peterson, David. *Thailand.* Danbury, Conn.: Scholastic Library, 2002.

Townsend, Sue. *A World of Recipes: Thailand.* Chicago: Heinemann Library, 2001.

An older reader can help you with this book:
Guile, Melanie. *Culture in Thailand.* Chicago: Raintree, 2003.

Glossary

agriculture growing of crops and raising of livestock

ancestor person you are related to who was born before you, like your mother, father, or grandparent

association group of people who have something in common and work together toward a goal

Buddhism religion based on teachings of a man known as Gautama or Buddha. He gave up his riches to become a monk.

culture ideas, skills, arts, and way of life for a certain group of people

cymbal musical instrument that is a metal disk. It is struck or hit against another cymbal.

daylight saving time when most Americans turn their clocks forward one hour in the spring and back one hour in the fall

degree title a student earns after finishing a program of study at a college or university

earthquake strong, shaking movement of the ground

employer person for whom someone works

folk having to do with the common people of a certain place. Folk music is the music played and written by the common people of an area.

heritage something passed down from one generation to the next

illegal immigrant person who is not allowed to live in a foreign country but who tries to anyway

immigrate to come to a country to live there for a long time. A person who immigrates is an immigrant.

martial arts fighting or self-defense sports or skills, such as judo, karate, or kung fu

monk member of religious group who promises to give up wealth, not get married, and obey the laws of a religion

settle to make a home for yourself and others

temple building used for worship and prayer

tradition belief or practice handed down through the years from one generation to the next

Vietnam War war fought from 1955 to 1975 between North and South Vietnam for the control of Vietnam. The United States fought for South Vietnam, but North Vietnam won control.

Index